Poetic

Encounters

with God

To Laura,

Aod Bless
you
and

Enjoy!

Andrea Turnbol
2/16/13

Poetic

Encounters

with God

Seeing God in Our Daily Walk

Andrea Turnboe

WinePressPublishing
Great Books, Defined.

WinePress Publishing (PO Box 428, Enumclaw, WA 98022) functions only as book publisher. As such, the ultimate design, content, editorial accuracy, and views expressed or implied in this work are those of the author.

All Scripture references are taken from the *King James Version* of the Bible.

ISBN 13: 978-1-4141-2136-9
ISBN 10: 1-4141-2136-9
Library of Congress Catalog Card Number: 2011932298

Dedication

To the Lord Jesus Christ, You have been
my strong tower and strength.

With heartfelt love to my father, Andrew,
and mother, Elizabeth Turnboe.

Contents

Part One: Encountering God

Appointed Time 1

Assured Presence 3

In His Presence 4

Amazing God 5

On Bended Knee 6

Connections 7

You Changed Me 8

Life Changed 9

Where Do I Fit? 10

Peace of Mind 11

The Field of Great Price 12

People of Purpose 13

Celebration of a Day 14

Imagination 15

He's Awake, You Know? 16

When Does God Speak? I 17

When Does God Speak? II 18

Part Two: Encountering Self and Others

I 21

Single Christian 22

Forty-two and Growing 23

Sleeping Giants 25

Try, Try, and Try Again 26

Watched Life 27

Love Birthed 28

The Greatest Find 29

The Mirror 30

War of Words 32

Dreams 33

Girlfriends 34

Part Three: Encountering Battles

Gigolo Man 37

The Morning After 39

The Last Dance 40

What He Took 41

Devil's Head 44

The Devil Revealed 45

The Unrepentant Soul 47

Angel's Fall 48

Anger – Let It Go 49

The Clown and the Crowd 50

He Has a Name 51

Not Defeated 53

When Life Has You Down 54

Directions 55

Mustard Seed Faith 56

Part Four: God's Intervention

The Grip of God 59

Change Me, God 60

David's Psalm 51 62

Rich Toward God 64

Would He Notice Me? 65

Jesus Lives! 67

The Truth 69

The Ordeal 70

Jesus's Plea 72

What God Can Do 74

Filled by the Holy Spirit. 76
Recruit Me, Holy Spirit 77
Close to God 78
Come a Little Closer 79
Rejoined. 80
Is Your Name Written Down? 81
Prayer for Salvation 83

About the Author. 85

Part One

Encountering God

Appointed Time

I'm drawn to You.
Drawn to hear Your voice,
To experience Your presence,
So I can know You.

As time ticks
So does my anticipation for You.
The hand of time moves.
My heart beats rhythmically,
As You draw me.

You arrive in confident majesty.
Gentleness issues from You as
I praise Your Holy Name.
You decorate my heart with Your essence.
You quietly speak in my spirit
And phrase words so purposefully,
Just for my hearing.

You are more than my anticipation.
More regal, more true, more beautiful.
You hold me with Your Word
And wrap comfort and strength around
My being, as under Your wing I find
Safety and warmth.

Appointed Time

Sweet communion we share,
As I see You once again as if
It were the first time.
New dimensions unfold.
Unrecognized perspectives of You
Are viewed.
Expressions flow from You
As you take me
To another level of You.

Life-changing procedures of the Holy Spirit
Change who I am,
Making me realize how much
I need to be more like You.
Must be and will be, as I submit to Your will.
I linger in Your presence.
I kneel before Your throne.
Wondering why I took so long to return to You.

Assured Presence

Wherever I go I'm assured of Your presence.
Like a beating pulse underneath the surface of skin,
You are there.
I'm aware of You, for I feel Your stirrings
And the impressions You make on my life are deep—
Deep like wells in springtime,
When I draw from You my substance.
You are real to me.
I remember a time in which I did
Not know You.
You know me, I'm Your beloved.
You draw me underneath Your wings
And I'm content there.
I adore You and wish my adoration to be known,
From my realm to Yours.
I bask in reverence of You.
Hallowing our time,
Knowing that we will never be apart,
For You intertwine my spirit
And position my heart in Your own,
Making us one.

In His Presence

I'm in that sacred place
Where the holy and the heart meet,
And where God kisses His creation.
I'm in the place
Where time no longer matters,
Where this season
Blends into more beautiful
Shades of reality.

I feel light
And see it too.
The once dark corners
Of my mind are brightened
By the rays of His love.

Grace prepared me
For this place.
As I surrendered my strivings
To the gentle pull on my heart
Toward Him.

I'm at peace now,
As I let Him lead me
In this walk of life.
A walk filled with His
Presence and favor.

Amazing God

I stand amazed at the wonder of the Lord.
His goodness knows no end,
His bounty is overflowing.
He is matchless and supreme,
None can compare with Him.
I cannot count all His benefits.
His grace is strong and sure.
All my days I'm reminded of how
Awesome He is, that none can
Outshine Him.
He smiles His favor upon me
And lifts me up when I stumble.
My life is engrafted in His hand.
I stand amazed at how much I am loved.

On Bended Knee

On bended knee I come,
Yielded, supple, and ready.
Ready to hear that familiar voice,
The one that spoke so gently to me
In the silence of the night and busyness of day.
The voice that reassured me
When I didn't know which way to turn,
Which way to go.
Words spoken to my heart that bring
Peace, calm, and a knowing.
A knowing that I'm not alone in this great place.
The universe cannot contain God,
Yet the miracle is He dwells in me.

How often I beat my chest,
Cried aloud and searched the heavens, looking.
All the while He was my next breath.
Connected to me like inner skin to soul,
Turning me, bending me, guiding me.
He flowed through me like water,
Illuminating and reflecting
The image I was made in.
So with bended heart I come
Ready to give Him the glory.
Because of Who He is, I am.
For without Him I'm
Reduced to dust, but with Him
I can do all things, for He is my helper.
He whispers silently His instructions
Taken from the master plan of His heart.

Connections

I'm here, though at times you don't feel me.
I care, though you may feel alone.
I hear you, though you may pray in whispers.
Your heart lies before me shown.
My heart tugs when you are crying,
For I am bound to you.
So don't feel deserted
Because I will see you through.

Your heart sighs within you.
Your pain is very great.
Be patient in your troubles
And I'll remove the weight.
Don't worry about tomorrow,
For I am the God of right now.
Your future is before me
And I will show you how.

So let peace be your companion,
For I am the Prince of Peace.
My comfort is reality
It will never cease.

You Changed Me

My heart was open for You to enter in.
So You did,
But only after I asked You.

You changed me from head to toe,
From heart to mind,
From soul to spirit.
But only after I let You.

I thought I knew what life was about.
Then You showed me.
You showed me You, then
Placed a mirror in front of me to
See if I matched.

I once was full of doubts, but You
Made me wiser,
For You are the truth.
Now I know.

You changed me for the better.
Now I have peace.
Thank You.

Life Changed

Like a silver glacier
With its heart of ice—
Cold and hard
Was I until the melting presence
Of the Son came upon me,
And drop by drop dissolved me.
Like a stone buried deep
In the earth,
You pressured me
Until I turned into
A stone-cutting diamond.
Like muddied water was I.
You, the spring of life, cleansed
The filth away and made me pure.

You are the life-changing power,
The means of righting a heart gone wrong.
You change the bad to good,
Change the unacceptable to the accepted
You turn willing lives into Your perfect plan.

Where Do I Fit?

Where do I fit in this world?
It's round,
I'm square.
It spins,
I'm unmovable.
Rotating on its axis, it changes.
Pushed down by gravity, I can't fly.
This world glides through space triumphant,
I walk cement-paved roads pondering things above.
Opposite entities—one free flowing,
The other glued in terrestrial's realm,
Oddly complement each other.
Like an apple falling from the tree,
I land on my knees seeking guidance.
Guidance from One Who orchestrated
Such refined motion in the heavens;
Who programmed perfect movement
In unthinking matter,
But Who also graced me to move in His Spirit.
Connected to the ultimate though rooted to earth.
I seek guidance that I may square right,
That I may fit in a space prepared for me and my kind.
This world is sustained by God's invisible hand.
I, however, am grafted in the same.
My being is filled with Him.
My countinence reflects His glory.
Where do I fit?
Right in the palm of His hand.

Peace of Mind

In humble abode I take my rest.
Like a bird upon its nest.
I lay weary head upon my palm,
Seeking a reassuring calm.
In this place I seek my peace,
Aware that confusion has ceased.
I close the door and my eyes.
Solace now I realize.
In my haven away from it all;
Peace is what this is called.
I wish this for the entire world.
As in my bed I lie curled.
Did I cause this on my own?
No, it is grace I feel to the bone.
God has given me peace of mind.
This is my lovely find.
Graciously imparted from above,
From a God of abundant love.

The Field of Great Price

Treasure deep was in its belly.
A find uncommon to naked eye.
Many men had traversed its dry ground unaware
Of its worth.
But a man of ancient wisdom appeared, who knew
The secret that went unseen for ages,
Knowledge that in its depths were rivers of oil.
Knowing its wealth, he gave all to secure this seemingly
Worthless field.

We are that dry field . . .
Dusty, walked upon, and unused.
To look upon the surface,
One asks, "Where is your value?"
However, God wants to deposit
The oil of the Holy Spirit within us.
This oil is priceless, for it is the
Abiding presence of God Himself.

The Holy Spirit woos our spirits for this filling.
Revealing to us that Jesus too gave up all,
His very life in order that we could become wells of life.
The treasure in the field is God.
We are His containers.
He is the One Who makes us useful
He is the One Who makes us full.
He comes in when we are empty and
Makes us of value.

People of Purpose

We are people of purpose on the rise.
We are people of purpose; we won't compromise.
We have a destiny issued from God's hand.
We will walk in His purpose, according to His plan.
We were known by God before the foundation of the earth.
It was then that our purpose was given birth.
People of God called to do a work in the land.
To speak boldly and take a stand
Against sin, which we see.
Yet we have much work to do and God to please.
But before we begin our task,
Let us bend our knees and ask
For the anointing of the Holy Spirit to overshadow us,
For to have His presence is a must.
As we encounter life in our homes or careers,
May we always have an attentive ear
To hear each word from the Lord
That we may always be in one accord
With one another and God most of all.
May we as God's people live up to the call
To spread the gospel in a godly way,
Making a difference for Christ each day.

Celebration of a Day

You have come to me
And I have embraced You.
This hour,
This day.
I savor You like fine cuisine,
Stretching the moments,
I relish Your flavor.
This is my day
Given to me,
Especially for me.
No two days have the same fingerprint.
For I was cast upon the shores of life
From the stream of God's heartbeat
To partake of life and be His reflection.
I look into the mirror and I see life.
I look at life and I see God all around.
God is in this day I celebrate.
I celebrate God for creating me to live it.

Imagination

Imagine a nation in your mind,
Your imagination.
Patriotic flair is inside you.
Your flag and standard right there.
This nation is so many things.
Combinations of thoughts inciting possibilities.
Ideas in beautiful colors and array standing strong.
A kaleidoscope nation flowing images through the brain.
So imagine a thing—
Imagine.
Reach deep in the mind and tap the ocean
Of vivid dreams there.
Let float to the surface a pool of possible reality.
There, there is no national guard to stop the flow.
Remind yourself to be mindful to
Concentrate on the incredible and bring to
Fruition the nation which is inside you—
God gave you imagination.

He's Awake, You Know?

There once was a lady who couldn't sleep a wink.
She would stare at the ceiling not giving a blink.
Throughout the night she would toss and turn.
Her unblinking eyes would start to burn.
This way and that, and back again,
This slumbering battle she could not win.
"Oh, if only I could have a moment's peace,
To allow my dreams to float and release.
My mind's so full of this day's course.
With all its cares I can't divorce
The many incidents that this day has brought,
I repeat them over, thought after thought."
Until suddenly, the thought miraculously occurred
Which made her sleeplessness seem absurd.
"God in heaven never slumbers or sleeps.
He watches over His children, their safety He keeps.
If God stays awake all night long,
I'm perfectly certain it won't be wrong
To close my eyes and drift away
So that tomorrow I can awaken to a brand new day.
While I sleep, to God I'll give my cares
And knowing how God works, tomorrow they won't even be there."
So the lady closed her eyes for a snooze,
Realizing, happily, that with God awake she had nothing to lose.

When Does God Speak? I

God speaks in the midnight hour.
This is the time He endues us with His power.
In the night season, when we're all alone,
God is building us and making us strong.
His calming voice speaks into the night
Making our problems to be all right.
His loving voice is what we need
To carry on and succeed.
So in the night, when we're perfectly still
Don't be surprised when we find God's will.
It's in the silence that His voice is heard.
He's moving our spirits into being stirred.
So when we hear a voice that's not so loud,
It may be God calling us away from the crowd.
Just quiet yourself and allow Him to speak,
As in His presence His face we seek.

When Does God Speak? II

God does not just speak in the midnight hour.
Throughout the day we can feel His power,
Guiding us, directing us according to the Bible,
Leading us into a season of great revival.
God's Word is the message that gets across the cross,
Restoring what had been forfeited and lost.
Communion with the Father because of His Son,
His sacrifice means we too have won.
He saved us from the weight of sin,
Allowing fellowship once again.
So talk to the Father throughout your day
He'll show you the path and the way.

Part Two

Encountering Self
and Others

I

I capitalize *I*
Because I'm important to me.
I stand alone
Just being me.

I capitalize *I*
Because I'm important in the world.
I'm uniquely special
Like a freshly discovered pearl.

I capitalize *I*
Because I'm special to God.
I come to Him boldly,
Without pretense or façade.

I know I have purpose,
A destiny to fulfill.
This purpose is encompassing.
I won't allow anyone to steal
My dreams or my day thoughts;
They are captured in my heart
For I know that I was given
Gifts and hope to impart.

So I capitalize *I*.
That is how it should be.
I can stand alone,
Because Jesus is with me.

Single Christian

Yes, I'm single; I'm without a mate.
Whether this is right or wrong, I won't debate.
I may be alone, but I'm definitely not lonely,
Because with God on my side, I'm not an "only."
As a single I can focus on pleasing the Lord.
Spending time with Him is a beautiful reward.
I can take this time and develop myself.
I'm being used of God; I'm not on the shelf.
I'm single and celibate, not giving in to sin.
I've decided to wait for marriage and not give in.
I'm walking step by step.
Singlehood for now I accept.
So I'm content in the station where I may be
A servant of Christ, I'm totally free!

Forty-two and Growing

I'm not over the hill,
Though I'm forty-two.
I'm kneeling at the cross,
Sending out prayers for you.

I'm not over and done with,
Barely making it to the end.
With morning devotions and prayers
Is how my day begins.

I'm a VIP special
I've got access to on high.
I check in regularly,
Don't let a day go by
Without connecting with the
Supreme God above.
It's through this connection
That I know of His wonderful love.

He has an important message
He wants me to communicate.
It comes just in time,
Never is it too late.

So listen to a message,
From a forty-two-year-old woman.
God loves you and wants you
To be part of His plan.

He knew you before the foundation
Of the earth.
Your destiny has had
An eternal birth.

Accept Jesus as the Savior
Of your life.
He'll forgive all your sin and
Remove all the strife.

Walk fully in the path set
Out for you.
Be born again and made
Completely new.

I'm forty-two and growing,
And my spirit will never die.
If you ask me how this could happen,
Jesus is the reason why.

Sleeping Giants

There once was a boy who loved to sleep.
His mother would call to him in the morning, saying,
"Wake up, boy! Wake up! Or you will miss your morning meal."
But the little boy slept on and of course missed the food that
Would sustain his body at school for the day.
When he did get to school, there too his teachers would
Find him asleep in his chair and say,
"Wake up, boy! Wake up! Or you will miss the lessons of life."
But the boy slept on and of course missed the food that
Would sustain his mind in the world. On Sunday mornings,
He would drag into church late and nod away
The sermon. The pastor would say,
"Wake up, boy! Wake up! Or you will miss the Lord knocking at your door."
But the boy slept on and missed the Lord asking entrance into his spirit.
The boy, however, one day did awake.
But he found that he was dead. His mind was as sharp
As a knife to this fact and that he was no longer a boy
But had died an old man with untapped potential.
He had slept his goals, abilities, and choices away. He had taken
Them all to his grave. His potential had remained asleep
In a world of multiple possibilities.

Try, Try, and Try Again

One hundred pairs of eyes, looking at me.
I am their focus, I'm what they see.
My knees quake beneath,
I hear my rattling teeth.
What must be said
Is floating around in my head.
Oh, to get this speech over is all I can do.
My lips form the words, but my tongue hasn't a clue
Of what to say to so many guests.
I guess I will just have to give it my best.
"Ladies and gentlemen," I finally say.
I find the words, my tongue will obey!
I continue my speech word after word.
To think I couldn't do this was simply absurd.
So try, try, and try again.
And remember, when you try, you always win.

Watched Life

His spirit, like a beacon,
Drew me.
I watched Him long
For many a year.
Yet He never knew
That my life depended on Him.
Always there, silently leading,
A steady light that did not diminish
No matter the storm.
No matter how harsh life tossed,
He remained firm
To the invisible eye watching,
Hoping that His was a stability
That would not crumble.
Watching—for chinks
In armored wall and cracks
That would let the flood tide in.
But chinks and cracks never existed,
They remained invisible.
All that remained was a towering
Strong man.

Love Birthed

Love birthed in the heart.
We now take part
Of a beautiful plan
Sent from God's open hand.

The bride has made herself ready
For the coming of her groom.
Like Christ coming in the eastern sky,
The bride has an appointment set from on high.

For a man takes woman
Here on this earth;
To love and cherish
And cultivate her worth.

Marriage is an example
For you and for me
Of our true relationship
With the holy He.

For marriage is a covenant
Sealed in love
An everlasting commitment,
As beautiful as two white doves.

From this time forth it is done
That you two will surely lean on God
A power stronger than you both
As you mature with love to full growth.

The Greatest Find

Love is a bond that knows no end.
Today I take you as my husband,
You've become more than friend.
In this marriage I give myself.
Being joined to you is worth
More than the world's wealth.

For in you I've found treasure galore.
And in each passing day I find even more.
I want to discover throughout all our years,
How to make you happy and abate your fears.

Together we will build a family that's secure,
For we are building on a foundation that is sure.
On Christ the solid rock we stand,
As we go through life hand in hand.

Know that I trust you to be my lead,
And in this marriage we will succeed.
Our marriage will stand the test of time,
For in you I found my rhyme.

The Mirror

There once was a girl whose skin was red, yellow, black, and white.
When people saw her they said, "Boy, what a sight!"
No one wanted to touch her; no one wanted her around.
What was to become of this girl in this town?

"No one likes me, of all the people I see.
No one loves me, which should not be.
I love everyone in the whole wide world.
But I'm sad because no one loves me, this lonely girl."

When she walked through town, people would stare.
Their eyes were something she could not bear.
They treated her as an "it" or some "thing."
But deep in her heart she knew she was a human being.

"The color of skin only goes skin deep.
It's the inside of a person that can make you weep.
Caught in four worlds of red, yellow, black, and white,
How do I ever make this thing right?

People caught up in what they see,
They never even recognize the real me.
How do I fit into a world when I'm both?
The colors accepted, the colors they loathe.

The Mirror

You've reduced me down to shades of myself
Treating me as if I was nothing else.
You've tried to leave me with shame.
Dare not you even ask my name?

Well, I'm not ashamed of who I may be.
For I am your reality.
I am the mirror that you must face,
When you chose to hate another race.

For you can't choose one shade of me to hate.
Your hating yourself is the weight.
So go ahead, ignore me still.
I am here, I am real."

War of Words

Lively battles for the mind,
Shooting thought-bullets across
The "mind" field.
War of words
Invade my thoughts, as I dodge
Phrases loaded with double meaning.
Hidden suggestions sneak underneath wired fences
Of resistances, as "mind" fields blow you out of reality.
Friendly fire has done more to sink confidence.
Are you ally or foe in this word game?
Or do your words indiscriminately mow down
All in your range?

Dreams

Dream Warrior, you tried to crush
My dreams and place them on your shelf.
But how do you view another's dreams
Another's impression of mind?
How do you draw it out?
With knife and scalpel or
Perhaps wire, glue, and plugs?
No tangible trace of me will show in your hand.
No scale will tip its weight to reveal my mysteries.
Heavy are my dreams, but you can't weigh them.
They're deeply buried in soulish forest.
You try to hunt and catch them in your nets,
But nets are not big enough to surround the dream mind.
My dreams are just too big.

Girlfriends

Shooting the breeze off the cuff,
After a day that has been so rough.
Laughing and talking and enjoying each other.
We're girlfriends, be it sister or mother.

We've gotten to know each other very well.
We could be sisters, who could tell?
You're my prayer partner when storms get bad.
We've cheered each other on until we're glad.
You're a part of me; you've had your effect.
Our friendship was called and elect.
You tell me the truth even when it hurts.
You're for real, never treating me like dirt.

Sharing conversations on the phone,
Being there when I'm alone.
I'm glad to have you as my friend.
I know our relationship will never end.
I will always cherish you for who you are.
You're my friend, you're my star.
Continue to grow, never stop
As together as friends we reach the top.

Part Three

Encountering Battles

Gigolo Man

Heart so blind
She didn't see him coming.
The gigolo man
Who just keeps on strumming.

All the signs were there
But she was blind to the fact
That she could have had
A man better than that.

He treated her well
For a little while,
Wooing her with his
White-toothed smile.

"You know I love you, baby."
Saying words she wanted to hear.
So she gave herself to him
Thinking that would keep him near.

But once he had gotten
Exactly what he wanted,
It was crystal clear where
All the signs were pointed.

Gigolo Man

He had his fill
And maybe a little bit more.
Then he crudely left her,
Walking out the door.

So beware of the gigolo man.
Face so pretty and teeth so grand.
Save your virtue for the wedding night.
Keep it pure. Do it right.

The Morning After

The tears flow as she cries, "Oh, no!
What have I done, my discontent has begun."
Overcome with her regret, she now carries a heavy debt.
The price of a one night stand, her virtue taken by some man.

"I thought I'd be happy if I had sex, but all I feel now is horribly vexed.
It didn't turn out the way I had planned, when I took part in this one
    night stand.
He said he loved me, but I now see in his eyes
That everything he said was a pack of lies.
I feel so used and cheaply low.
Where can I hide? Where can I go?"
Her expressions of love are now expressions of regret
As she discovers her desires have gone unmet.

God says that the man who finds a wife finds a good thing.
So remember before you act to wait for the wedding ring.
In the covenant of marriage there's no reason for shame.
Your love is then real and not some game.
So continue to wait for your special mate.
It's worth the time and worth the wait.

The Last Dance

She swung from partner to partner
Holding them close to her.
Digging into the sway, sleek and classy.
She liked the way this one moved, masculine not sassy.
Evening after evening she danced her life away.
Indiscriminate of whom, she had no forte.
However, the racier the better,
As man and woman danced together.

She shared her love here and there.
She wasn't partial, she didn't care.
Until one night she danced with Disease.
All her free love came to a freeze.
He looked no less charming than all the rest.
Until later when she took the HIV test.
The test came back positive in her case,
Her results impossible to erase.

No longer was she footloose and fancy free.
No longer the life of the party.
This partner had claimed his dance
And didn't leave her with a second chance.

What He Took

He sought innocence under an oak tree,
When she was young and naive.
She gave him all her love,
She was so eager to please.

He took her love that night
Then went along his way.
When she saw him again,
He had nothing to say.

She said, "Do you take hearts so easily
And blast them apart?
Was this your plan
From the very start?

I deserve an answer
For being treated in such a way.
Don't remain silent,
What do you have to say?"

He replied, "Since you insist,
Then I'll explain my actions to you.
Yes, this is my *modus operandi*
This thing that I do.

What He Took

"I'm a smooth operator,"
Is what he said.
"My goal that night
Was to get you in my bed.

You're just another number
In my notched belt.
When I had sex with you,
It wasn't love I felt.

You see, I've made an agreement
With the devil himself,
That if I deflowered virgins
He would give me wealth.

You mean nothing to me.
You're just a means to my end.
We were never true lovers,
I'm not even your friend."

She replied, "So I'm just another
You've corrupted in your path.
You plan to leave me now
In the rubble of the aftermath.

But I'm a stronger person
Than what you think.
Now I'm aware of you,
I won't further sink.

What He Took

I asked God for forgiveness
For what I have done.
For I gave my body away
And didn't wait for the true one.

So I'll warn others virgins
That there are men like you.
I won't make it easy
For this thing that you do.

Through my tragedy,
I'll fight you, demon of hell,
And to every willing woman's ear
My story I will gladly tell.

I'll live to know that I saved
Another from your vice.
I'll see all your notches melt
Away like ice.

I'll tell every woman to wait
For a marriage ring.
To be given away as a princess
By her heavenly Father, the King of Kings.

Make a family as a husband and wife
And share true love throughout their life."
From that moment a contest of wills begins,
Now it is up to you to take a stand and win!

Devil's Head

The devil will rear his head,
But through Jesus Christ the devil's work is rendered dead!

The Devil Revealed

I sit here and wait
For you to take my bait.
I devise your fall,
Such misery and all.
All you need do is give in
And nurture your sin.
Drink my poison down
Then I've won this round.
My main thought is your demise
You, I will always criticize.
I see nothing good in your life.
I want to prick you with the sting of strife.
If I could get you to see things my way
Then nothing good will you ever have to say.
I want to snatch you away from Christ.
To accomplish this I'll use any device.
Don't read the Word or that Bible stuff.
Be full of worry until you've had enough.
Don't follow rules, do your own thing
And we'll see what kind of results this will bring.
I want to control your mind
Until there is no happiness inside.
Up front I don't tell you these things
Only later when there's no hope in your wings.
I'm your friend for now; we're walking side by side!
Just follow me; I'll be your guide.

I'll hang around and become hauntingly familiar
Until my presence is no longer peculiar.
I'm very clever and I know how to wait
Sooner or later you'll take my bait.
So I leave you with pick and shovel.
Signing off,
Sincerely, the devil

The Unrepentant Soul

I was not confused.
I knew my actions from start to finish.
Now I am alone,
My hope diminished.
Tortured dreams
And a hectic life
My heart was darkened
I was full of strife.
Death's hand had passed my way.
Now I am trapped in a pit of decay.
I am buried under grave's shadow.
Life a lost battle.

A lost soul barreling down . . . down . . . down.
Defeated, crying without sound.
My voice unable to speak,
Agony had reached its peak.
Misery untold etched in my being,
But all the while I knew its meaning.
I had placed myself here by my choice.
My decision in life had been my voice.

Angel's Fall

My eternal unrest was not by fate,
For in my heart, God I did hate.
I had warred with Him by my own choosing.
Fighting Christ, I knew I was losing.
Yet I continued in my pride.
I, myself, would have pierced His side.
For I wanted Him dead and not exalted.
His very throne I too assaulted.
For my rebellion was like the start,
Archangel and God now forever apart.
My separation began on earth,
Then continues in the Lake of Fire, for I am cursed.
This separation I cannot undo
Because of the pride I did pursue.

Anger – Let It Go

Anger packed down
Like an overstuffed hamper
Leaving no room to maneuver,
Just a crumpled life.

The Clown and the Crowd

The clown wept alone
Then went to laugh for the crowd,
Frown masked as glee.
No one noticed his pain.
Caught up in the surface emotion,
The crowd laughed,
Hiding too their insides.
Crowd and clown, mirrors
Of each other.
Neither telling the truth.
Both in pain,
Both wearing a smile.

He Has a Name

They call him Sammy,
The man in front of the store.
He reaches for the bottle once more.
Hour upon hour, he sits in the streets,
Asking for nickels and dimes from those he meets.
He gradually drinks his life away,
His liver quickly turning to decay.

They call him Mr. Rozini,
The neighbor next door.
He reaches for a martini once more.
Hour upon hour he drinks at the bar,
Before leaving, bleary-eyed, in his car.
He gradually drinks his life away,
He drives facing disaster along the way.

They call him Dad,
The man coming through the door.
He reaches for a beer once more.
Hour upon hour he will sit in his chair,
And ramble on into crowded air.
He gradually drinks his life away.
His family, seeing only grey.

He Has a Name

He could be called by any name.
His destructive acts are just the same.
This drunken man in our lives,
Who terrorizes neighborhoods, children, and wives.
He's not just someone without a name,
But a father, a brother, an uncle—what a shame.
Alcoholism has a face,
And on it, the smile is erased.

Not Defeated

I put years in on this job, now it is completed.
No longer there, but I am not defeated.
This job may be coming to an end,
But there's more for me around the bend.
Admittedly, I'm a little discouraged, a little upset.
However, with God on my side, I don't have to fret.
This transition is just a change.
My life's being reordered, being rearranged.
God knew about this from the beginning.
I'm about to start something new; it's not an ending.
Nothing catches God by surprise.
I'm his child so I realize
That I'm in His perfect will.
So I calm myself, I am still.
I will take one step at a time.
It may not be easy, but I'm willing to climb.
Either way, I am prepared
To start again, I refuse to be scared.
I know up ahead and to the right,
There will be a shining light
For me to tightly grab ahold
And lift up high and bold.
It will guide me as this change appears,
But with God as my light I have nothing to fear.

When Life Has You Down

What in the world
Do I have left
When I've hung up the gloves,
And I am on the shelf?
Trying to get by on what I used to be,
Walking down the street, no one recognizes me.
I used to be on the top of my game.
But things happened; I'm no longer the same.
Some call me a loser; others say I've met defeat.
While others say that the world's got me beat.
It's in these times of the very low of low
That I speak to my soul and let it know
That it's not circumstances that makes a woman or man
But how in those times they stand.
I've been successful many times before,
I know I can be successful once more.
I'm not going to listen to the blues or that rap,
It defeats the purpose; I'll change what is in my lap.
If life gives you lemons, sell lemonade.
I'm unique, I'm handmade.
I'm grafted upon the palm of God's hand.
I'll soon be back in demand.
But even if not, God will take care of His child.
Knowing this, I can go the distance mile after mile.
I'm not about to give up. I have too much in store.
I'm going higher, farther, and much, much more.

Directions

I was torn with emotions
That raged through my mind.
I was lost in indecision,
A path I could not find.
I was walking in darkness
Unable to see
What traps and ditches
Were before me.
In which direction do I chart my course?
What path to take without having remorse?
I hesitated to fall in the pits on land,
Prayed deeply for a helping hand.
If I had God's guidance I would surely know
In which direction I'm predestined to go.
Again I bowed my head and prayed to the Lord,
Releasing all the fears I hoard.
Years of fears were released from my depths,
Allowing me to take confident steps
In the direction I should go.
This the Lord my God did gladly show.
He took me away from the constant fear
And reassured me that He was near.
Knowing now that God was truly on my side
My eyes are open very wide
To the fact that with God in my affairs
There will never be anything too hard to bear.

Mustard Seed Faith

Doubt, like a worm, inches
Its way through my mind,
Nibbling my faith,
Placing it on test.
Putting on the scales of trust and uncertainty,
Questions of loyalty arise.
Questions of my existence surface.
However, I recall that what is unseen is
More powerful than the seen,
The invisible holding the visible together.
Microscopic words creating life and matter.
My faith, now like a mustard seed, is small.
But it has enough energy to move
This mountain of doubt
Into the sea of non-remembrance.
Heavy, like brick, are these seeds.
Tilting the balance in my favor.
Faith roots, and like a giant tree
Branches wide to model my faith.
A grain of seed igniting my world.

Part Four

God's Intervention

The Grip of God

The grip of God
Is like a strong tower,
Sure and secure.

The touch of the Holy Spirit
Is calm and assuring,
For He is the Comforter.

The breath of God
Blows fresh renewal upon His people,
For He is the breath of life.

The voice of God
Is living and powerful,
Speaking into existence His mind.

But the love of God
Reaches down to filthy man
And cleans him with the tears of His blood
Then gives to man a new heart, if only man
Will ask.

Change Me, God

How do I change this self who I am?
This lion of a self, nothing like a lamb?
I see the glaring faults that surround me wide.
These many faults that always abide.

"I'm the source of change in your life.
I can free you from the all-consuming vice.
You are the mirror that will reflect
My glory. Do not reject."

But how can this earthen vessel reveal
The glory you instill?
I'm so easy to break; I'm not strong at all.
Yet inside I have build up a wall.

"This wall inside is easy to tear down.
And in its place will be hallow ground.
Just come daily into my midst.
And gradually your troubled mind will be fixed."

Oh, yes, Lord, I want this wall torn down.
To have peace of mind that is sound.
Free me from all-consuming vices
And show me where true life is.

Change Me, God

"If you have the willing heart to admit
That on your own you cannot quit,
But need the assistance that I give
Then I assure you that you shall live."

My God, I lean on You
And trust that You will see me through.
With all my faults, I can be completely free
Because I know that You dwell in me.

"I forgive you for all your sin.
With Me, new life will begin.
Just talk to Me and open up
And I will more than fill your cup.
Don't be afraid to let go.
Step on out into the overflow.
I'm the great loving God,
So remember with me to be shod."

David's Psalm 51

The sacrifice of God is a broken spirit
This sacrifice, He will hear it.
A heart that is broken and contrite
This is the way to be positioned right.

A heart like this He will not despise,
For it is a heart that cries.
Cries out for sin to be erased,
To be lifted up, no longer debased.

In Thy good pleasure do good unto Zion.
The walls of Jerusalem build, O Judah's Lion.
O God, deliver me from guiltiness.
My tongue shall magnify Thy righteousness.

Only You can create in me a clean heart.
Only You have the right spirit to impart.
Never banish me from Your precious presence.
Keep Your Holy Spirit in residence.

May my salvation be restored.
Uphold me as Your Holy Spirit is freely outpoured.
Only through Your Spirit can I teach transgressors Thy way.
And sinners shall be converted to willingly obey.

David's Psalm 51

My lips will praise Thee all the day long.
Not in burnt offering but in delightful song.
That is true worship given from my being.
The inner man worships for God's seeing.

Sacrifice righteousness before the King of Kings
Then He will show you what offerings to bring.
Pleasing God is what it is all about.
Praising God through purity upon His Holy Spirit mount.
So lift up holy hands to the Lord Most High.
Praise and worship are continuous; they will never die.

Rich Toward God

Teach me, Lord, to be rich toward You.
Is it in money or attitude?
Do I give of myself and my time?
Or am I always on the getting climb?
Share true wealth, which is the Word of God.
Use His standard as the real measuring rod.
Isn't this the standard that reveals true value?
Not paper and gold or what have you.
What's printed on paper or what's on the heart,
Both can impart.
However, I choose today the One to Whom I'll be loyal.
I choose Jesus—He is my all in all, the royal.
He is my sustainer, He upholds me in His hand.
And that is worth more than a trillion grand.

Would He Notice Me?

If Jesus walked the earth today
And happened to pass my way,
Would He notice me?
For I'm so quiet and timid
Would He give a minute
To notice me?
With so many others in dire need
Asking Him for a miracle deed,
Would He notice me?
Way in the back away from Him
In the shadows dim,
Would He notice me?
So many crowding around Him, competing for His hand
All pressing in to touch this Savior, the Son of Man.
Others are so eloquent and speak with flowery words.
My speech is anguished, like a wounded, fallen bird.
I'm not important or commanding
I can barely raise my eyes.
My heart is very heavy; my prayers come out as sighs.
Would Jesus notice someone like me?
Would He turn his gaze to set me free?

I found the answer to that question to be most definitely, "Yes."
I, that wounded bird that had fallen from its nest,
Can rest assured beyond a shadow of a doubt
That Jesus Christ had worked it out.

Would He Notice Me?

He knew there would be many like me,
Who had an anguished plea.
Multitudes would cry out to Him
And Jesus Christ would answer all of them.

The Holy Spirit, the third person of the Godhead,
Would help us to be God led.
God in every moment of my day.
Indwelling me in a very special way.
I have God's attention all the day long
And with Him in me I can grow very strong.
God knew me before the foundation of the earth.
And sent the Holy Spirit to initiate my new birth.
No longer must I hide on the fringes of the crowd.
Now I can pray quietly or pray aloud.

Jesus Lives!

Jesus lived two thousand years ago,
But He is not two thousand years away.
He healed the afflicted long ago,
But His touch can still heal today.
Wounded, bruised, battered, and scarred,
Rejected, misunderstood, and marred
Was Jesus on the cross that day,
In order that His death would provide a way
For man to be justified before God.
This is real and not a façade.
Because of the cross everyone can flock to Jesus's care,
Receiving forgiveness for sin, a burden no one can bear,
Like many, I too was once wounded, crushed under sin.
My world was a darkened, oblique den.
My heart so cold, embittered, and filled with hate.
Anger crippled me like an unyielding weight.
I needed a Savior, someone Who could set me free.
And eradicate the emptiness that plagued me.

I looked high and low for so many years.
When the Holy Spirit revealed Jesus I cried repentant tears.
God knew me long before I began to search.
It was He Who decreed that I now belong to the Church.
Jesus now fills the void that was once deep within my being.
His inspiring Word brought understanding to my seeing.
His peace drove terror away from my soul
And brought His warmth of love eliminating the cold.

Jesus Lives!

So though Jesus lived two thousand years ago,
He now reigns as resurrected Lord and wants everyone to know
That they too can be free of sin and have God's peace.
Just acknowledge Him as Savior and the war will cease.
Because of Jesus's death and resurrection for man,
We're no longer enemies of God but proclaimed His friends.

The Truth

Seeking minds need to know,
So they endeavor, if need be, to go
To the furthest ends to discover truth.
But is truth so distant, so far away?
Pilate once asked Jesus, "What is truth?"
Not knowing he was face to face with the answer.
The truth has stood at the heart of many men and knocked.

The truth is a person, the Christ, the Messiah.
The truth is the Son of God revealed.
He shows you the Father and your need for reconnection.
The truth stands tall for every man to accept.
What will you do when you meet the truth?

The Ordeal

They took a righteous man,
Placed Him upon a stand.
They accused Him to His face,
Tried to make Him a disgrace.

Mocked and tormented,
But He never once relented.
Stripes upon His back
Given at whip's crack.

His body took a beating.
The memory is not fleeting.
Nails in each hand.
The pain, who could stand?

Pain that is extreme.
God knowing what it means.
Pierced in His side
He had already died.

Placed in a stone tomb,
Joseph making room.
Spirit and soul descending down
Into the center of the ground.

The Ordeal

Preached there to souls which were departed.
Victory over death He imparted,
On the third day He arose to the living.
Abundant grace He keeps on giving.

Now seated at the right hand of the Father.
No need of ours too great to bother.
We now have access to the One on high.
For Jesus is the reason why.

Jesus's Plea

Throw open the door
And welcome Me inside.
My blood had broken
And destroyed the locks.
The locks are useless now,
No longer separating us.

Throw open the door
And let Me walk through.
The barriers are removed and broken down.
The only barrier now
Is you.

Throw open the door.
Allow Me to enter in.
I'm so close,
So near.
Reach out and touch all you once wanted
But didn't know you could have.
Now I'm yours.
Just throw open the door.
I'm on the other side.
Waiting to access
Your home, your heart.
Just let Me in.

Jesus's Plea

I've waited with expectant
Patience.
Now is the time.
Don't wait any longer.
Just open the door
Let us have fellowship together,
And I'll never depart.

What God Can Do

Wretched—wretched and undone,
He bowed before the Holy One.
Filthy rags draped his being,
Before anyone else, he would have felt like fleeing.
He had come to the end of himself,
Poor, cast down, without a shred of spiritual wealth.
Before the Lord he bowed,
Just he and God alone, no crowd.
God, so righteous, looked upon him.
Yet this poor soul He did not condemn.
For this soul had called out for grace.
The blood of Jesus, now on him, couldn't be erased.
No longer wretched, he was made upright,
His sins forgiven, his heart no longer black as night.
A transformation was performed
As this man became new born.
He was cleansed from head to foot.
Embedded sin God did uproot.
God washed his soul, spirit, and mind.
No more dregs and no more grime.

His filthy rags were exchanged for a royal robe.
Nothing like it could be found on earthy globe.
For he had put on Christ
And rid himself of Satan's vice.
He was made into a new creation.
There was no more speculation,
Reality had set in.

What God Can Do

He has been saved from sin.
He found his purpose spoken before the foundation of the earth.
He had experienced the new birth.
All of heaven's angels joined in to sing
For the one who had been reunited with the King of Kings.
No longer wretched, downcast, and low,
But uplifted and high—gloriously so.
So for those wretched and undone,
Come and bow before the Holy One.
No sin is too great.
Open your heart—don't wait.

Filled by the Holy Spirit

The Holy Spirit blew on my spirit
And I spoke with heavenly tongues.
Like living water I was freed.
I was baptized with an infilling so rich,
I never wanted to leave.
A baptism so encompassing that my spirit
Felt the fullness of God.
A new language, a godly language,
Unique for His hearing bypassed
My mind and danced with the spiritual.
My spirit joining God's in one conversation,
Until I spoke a sweet language melody from above:
A speech so clear and so pure—
It is higher even than the ancient godly Hebrew.
Angels entertained theses utterances,
But God inspired the words.
The syllables and sounds resonated from within my being.
Terrestrial ears don't understand such flow.
Some even mock.
But God's infilling is a blessed miracle that is communication prayer.
It is my spirit praying when I cannot find the words.
It is a continual miracle experience that can be enjoyed
all the days of my life.

Recruit Me, Holy Spirit

Recruit me, Holy Spirit.
I want to do what You want me to.
Recruit me, Holy Spirit
To seek after what You want me to pursue.
May I be an example in this world
Of Your tender grace.
May I be an example to others,
No matter the race.
Teach me to love my fellow man,
To show Christ's love and to be on hand,
Watching and praying for people's release,
Letting them know that they can have peace.
Recruit me to kindness and a gentle word,
To put in action all that I have heard.
Use my life as a witnessing device,
For I know Your power will more than suffice.

Close to God

God, thank You for all You have done for me, Your child.
I come into Your presence to be with You for awhile.
If I could, I would wrap my arms around You.
Just abiding in Your love is what I want to do.
I wish to be the apple of Your eye.
That is my longing, that is my cry.
I want to be close to Your heart,
Listening daily to instructions You impart.
I'm so glad to be under Your wing.
From this position I will continuously sing.
You said You'll be with me every day.
So I know that from Your love I cannot stray.
I thank You, God, for loving me.
I'll worship You in word, action, and deed.

Come a Little Closer

Come a little closer,
I want you to be near.
Come a little closer
For you are so dear.

Don't pull back from Me
You are dear to My heart.
Don't pull back from Me
I have so much to impart.

Just open up a little
I will show you the world.
Just open up a little
There's no need to curl.

Freedom to enjoy My love
Is what I'm giving to you.
Freedom to enjoy My peace,
This peace you no longer have to pursue.

So come a little closer
I have so much to give.
Come a little closer
And really start to live.

Rejoined

Man and God visually united
Because of choices they both decided.
Christ's decision to die upon splintered wood,
To give His life so man could
Spend eternity in heavenly glory.
Man now having a new story,
Only if man chooses to accept Christ
And welcome Him into his life.
Sin is no longer remembered,
More than a life that has been reconfigured.
Having eternal communion once again
Without the burden of sin.
Heavenly joy all day long,
No night, just peaceful song.
Man's voice joined to heavenly harmony.
No more war, no more army.
A time to be who man is supposed to be.
For all evil will bow its knee.
Judgment executed on the head of the devil.
He is brought down, no longer a rebel.
Now man joined back to God's heart
In eternity, never to depart.

Is Your Name Written Down?

When the Book of Life is opened,
Will your name be found within?
Are you among the redeemed ones?
Has your life been forgiven of sin?

When God looks down that column,
Will your name be in print?
Is your name written down in glory
Because you did repent?

Or will there be another tale
Of sin not abated?
How you never allowed Jesus in
Throughout your earthly day?

But how you lived for yourself,
Ignoring God's call?
Never being resurrected,
But remaining in the fall?

Never asking for your name
To be included in the Book of Life,
But remaining in sin
With all your strife?

Is Your Name Written Down?

Answer the call,
Sent from God above.
It is a call of favor,
It is a call of love.

Develop a relationship with Elohim.
He will show you what life means.
Stop ignoring the knocking at your heart's door.
Because one day the knocking will be no more.

Open up while you have the chance
To enjoy this spiritual romance.
It's not too late; you still have breath inside.
Choose Jesus; on Him decide.

Prayer for Salvation

Dear Heavenly Father,

I ask that You come into my life and save me and give me new life. I acknowledge that I am a sinner and cannot save myself. I repent and ask for forgiveness of my sins. I thank You that You sent Your Son Jesus Christ to come and die on the cross at Calvary's hill in order to redeem me. I thank You for the cleansing blood of the Lord Jesus Christ that washes away my sin. I also thank You for Your wonder-working power that raised Christ from the dead, and I now ask for the Lord Jesus Christ and the Holy Spirit to come and dwell within me. I thank You for a new beginning in You, and I will live my life through the Holy Spirit of God for Your glory. I thank You for Your continued presence and that my encounter with You is everlasting.

In the name of the Lord Jesus Christ,
Amen

That if thou shall confess with thy mouth the Lord Jesus, and shall believe in thine heart that God hath raised him from the dead, thou shalt be saved.

—Romans 10:9

For God so loved the world, that he gave his only begotten Son, that whosoever believeth in him should not perish, but have everlasting life.

—John 3:16

About the Author

Andrea Turnboe gave her life to Christ at an early age and attended Christian Education in her formative years. Her previous book, *Poetic Pearls,* was published in 2006 and deals with the pressure of life and how God can make you into rare treasure. She has a degree in communications from University of Detroit Mercy and a master's degree in liberal studies from UDM.

CPSIA information can be obtained at www.ICGtesting.com
Printed in the USA
BVOW030425201212

308719BV00001B/20/P